Walt Disney World®

CRESCENT BOOKS
NEW YORK

CLB 1357
© 1985 Illustrations: Walt Disney Productions.
© 1985 Text: Colour Library Books Ltd., Guildford, Surrey, Engla
Text filmsetting by Acesetters Ltd., Richmond, Surrey, England.
Printed in Spain.
All rights reserved.
1985 edition published by Crescent Books, distributed
by Crown Publishers, Inc.
ISBN 0-517-48085-9
h g f e d c b a

Following the unqualified success of his first Magic Kingdom, Disneyland, Walt Disney quickly realized the potential that existed for a second kingdom to serve the eastern states of America. This time, however, he wanted it to be on a larger scale – a complete vacationland – something he had not been able to achieve in California because of lack of space.

For his new venture he chose Florida. Its climate, similar to that of Southern California, would ensure year-round operation, and it already had a thriving tourist industry.

By October 1965, 27,443-acres of pine forest in the heart of America's sunshine state had been purchased, at a cost of just over five million dollars, and by 1970, at the peak of construction, Walt Disney World was easily the largest private building project in the United States, if not the world.

It included the creation of a 200-acre lake, to be named the Seven Seas Lagoon, which was connected to the beautiful, natural Bay Lake by a concrete channel. White sand was used to make sumptuous beaches, and hundreds of palm trees were planted to form an idyllic setting for the Polynesian Resort Hotel. Another luxury hotel, the Contemporary Resort, was built overlooking both the lagoon and Bay Lake. This hotel makes a fitting backdrop for Tomorrowland, one of the themed areas of the Magic Kingdom, the others being: Main Street U.S.A., Adventureland, Frontierland, Liberty Square and Fantasyland. In addition, shops and restaurants were built catering for every taste.

To provide electricity and hot water for heating and cooking systems for the hotels and Magic Kingdom, a central energy plant was specially constructed. In order to maintain the required high standards of cleanliness, a unique trash collection system – AVAC – was installed and, to prevent flooding, forty miles of canals were incorporated into Walt Disney World's ambitious plans.

A vast collection of "ingredients" for the park were brought from all over the world: huge monorail beams from Washington State, old steam locomotives from Mexico, gas turbines from Canada, cables and towers from Switzerland, and even wigs from Guatemala.

On the sporting side, the facilities of Walt Disney World are superb. There are two championship golf courses, boating on a variety of water craft, tennis, water skiing, and nature trails for hiking or horseback riding in the beautiful countryside.

Walt Disney had been an ardent conservationist and he was particularly concerned that the ecological balance of the land he had bought should be disturbed as little as possible. Too much of Florida had been spoilt by past developers and he therefore designated 7,500-acres as a nature reserve; an area of virgin swamp and hardwood forest where wildlife could remain undisturbed.

On October 1st, 1971, Roy Disney proudly dedicated Walt Disney World to the memory of his brother and "to the talents, the dedication and the loyalty of the entire Disney organization that made Walt Disney's dream come true. May Walt Disney World bring joy and inspiration and new knowledge to all who come to this happy place... a Magic Kingdom where the young at heart of all ages can laugh and play and learn – together."

As proof of how right had been Walt Disney's judgement, 10.8 million people visited the park in its first year. This response was enough to encourage the Disney organization to launch a 200 million dollar expansion program.

Since that time, another project within Walt Disney World has reached fruition. It goes by the name Epcot Center – an Experimental Prototype Community of Tomorrow – and was another of Walt Disney's long-cherished ideas. More than twice the size of the Walt Disney World Magic Kingdom, Epcot Center consists of two exciting dimensions: Future World, in which may be explored new ideas and innovations in communications, energy and transportation, and where visitors can discover how the dreams of today can become the realities of tomorrow, and World Showcase, in which nine nations open their doors, sharing their accomplishments and cultures in exciting shows, attractions, restaurants and shops unique to each country. Epcot is, indeed, fulfilling the prediction of Walt Disney, that it would become a place that "more people would talk about and come to look at than any other place in the world" – a combination of the creative imagination of the Disney organization and the technical skills of American industry.

Previous page: a parade on Main Street.
Facing page: Alice, the Walrus and the White Rabbit outside Cinderella Castle.

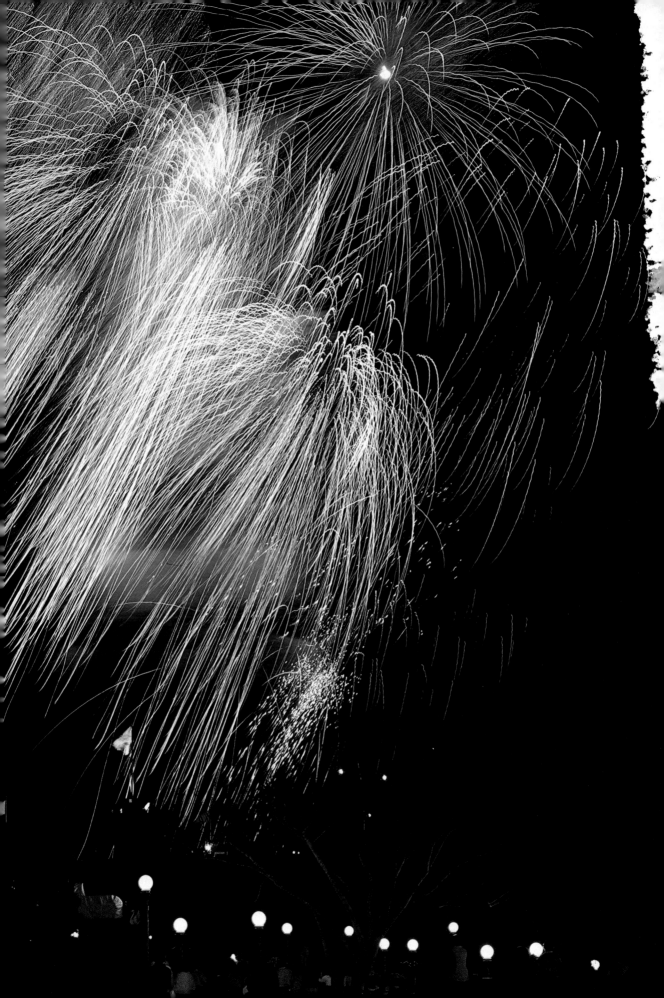

Previous pages: a firework display and an illuminated Cinderella Castle. Top left: a romantic evening cruise on the *Admiral Joe Fowler* in Frontierland. Top center: Mickey Mouse. Top right: the Davy Crockett explorer canoe travels toward Tom Sawyer Island. Above: Main Street. Left: Alice, the Walrus and the White Rabbit greet young visitors. Overleaf: the exciting StarJets in Tomorrowland.

ft: the Jungle Cruise in
dventureland. Far left: sailing
the Polynesian Village. Top
ft: Pinocchio, Mickey Mouse and
onald Duck. Above: the nightshow
the Polynesian Village. Top
nter: one of the sternwheelers
Liberty Square. Top right: the
nshine Pavilion. Right: a horse
r and Cinderella Castle.
erleaf: Cinderella Castle with
set left) Mickey Mouse and
set right) Donald Duck.

eft: a military parade in
iberty Square. Top left: a
arade in Main Street. Above: the
onorail train leaves the
ontemporary Resort Hotel. Top:
e lights which illuminate the
ernwheelers around Tom Sawyer's
land at nighttime. Right:
igger entertains a visitor.
verleaf: Cinderella Castle.

Facing page: Mickey Mouse and Cinderella Castle. Top: the Contemporary Resort Hotel. Left: a parade on Main Street. Above: Roy Disney and Mickey Mouse. Overleaf: the Crystal Palace Restaurant.

Left: Donald Duck and friends on Main Street. Top: Walt Disney World Railroad near Tom Sawyer Island. Above: the exciting Dumbo, the Flying Elephant ride. Facing page: Cinderella Castle. Overleaf: the Riverboat Landing, Liberty Square.

Left: Mickey Mouse plays golf on one of the links at the Golf Resort Hotel (right). Top right: the Contemporary Resort Hotel. Top: City Hall, on Town Square. Above a scene from the Jungle Cruise. Overleaf: Main Street

Top left: 20,000 Leagues Under the
Sea, in Fantasyland. Top right: a
paddlewheeler at the Contemporary
Resort. Above: elephants and (left)
hippopotamuses on the Jungle Cruise.
Far left: Cinderella Castle.
Overleaf: the Polynesian Village.

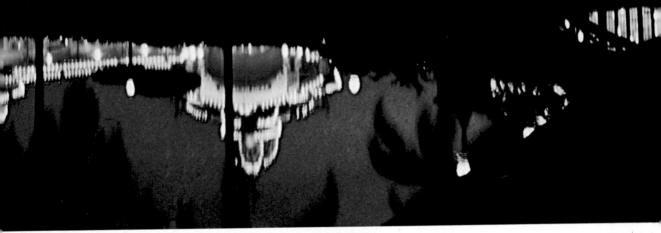

Top left: Brer Fox. Top right: Crystal Palace. Above: Mickey Mouse. Left: River Country. Far left: Walt Disney World Railroad. Overleaf: (top left) Main Street; (bottom left) Main Street Railroad Station and (right) Cinderella Castle.

Left: the exciting runaway train of the Big Thunder
Mountain Railroad. Top: the soaring StarJets and the
Space Mountain beyond. Above: a motor bus and (fac
page bottom) a horse car in Main Street. Facing page
top: hippopotamuses threaten the launch on the Jun
Cruise.

Left: the monorail train glides through the spectacular foyer of the Contemporary Resort Hotel. Above: Tree House Villas. Top: the swimming facilities of River Country. Facing page top: Contemporary Resort Hotel. Facing page bottom: Polynesian Village Resort. Overleaf: the *Empress Lilly* riverboat on Lake Buena Vista.

Facing page: Tigger outside Cinderella Castle. Below: a mass of blooms in Main Street. Bottom: some of the seven dwarfs. Right and bottom right: the steam-powered *Admiral Joe Fowler* cruises past Tom Sawyer Island.

Top left: Golf Resort. Left: the *Empress Lilly*, a replica of a Mississippi sternwheeler. Top: Cinderella Castle. Above: Contemporary Resort.

Top: the Canada section of the World Showcase at EPCOT Center. Remaining pictures: the American Adventure at the EPCOT Center, where Benjamin Franklin (above) leads a cast of audio-animatronics and humans in a vivid re-creation of American history.

Above and overleaf bottom right: the 18-story geosphere at the Spaceship Earth, within EPCOT's Future World, where the importance of communication in the development of civilization is explained. Remaining pictures: the impressive prehistoric dinosaurs which confront visitors to the Universe of Energy (overleaf top right) at the EPCOT Center. Overleaf: (left) the monorail glides past Journey into Imagination.

These pages and overleaf: cultural contrasts to be seen at the World Showcase. This page: Japan with its pagoda. Facing page: Germany with its alpenhorn players. Overleaf: (top left) France; (bottom left and top right) Italy and (bottom center and bottom right) the United Kingdom.

These pages: at the EPCOT Center, elaborate displays show how life in the future may develop. Overleaf: the World Showcase: (top left and bottom left) China; (bottom center) Mexico and (top and bottom right) Morocco, one of the newest additions to the center.

Top: an artist's impression of a coming attraction at the EPCOT Center. Left: one of the more futuristic exhibits at EPCOT's World of Motion presentation. Remaining pictures scenes from the Journey into Imagination. Overleaf: Cinderella Castle.

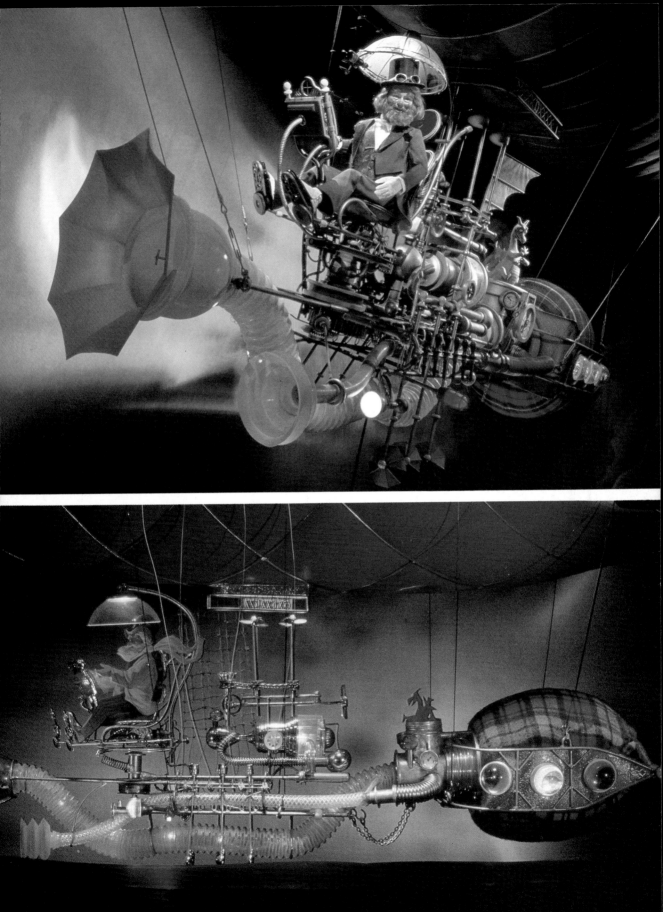